# *Praise for The Golden Handoff Workbook*

"In my 40+ years in the real estate business, I've seen countless training manuals, books and guides. Although there are many that offer valuable content, there typically is one missing ingredient. Specific direction! The industry is known for providing good, solid ideas, but much more often than not, it leaves the reader trying to figure out on their own, exactly what steps to take in order to experience success with the information. What Nick Krautter has done in this workbook is provide that missing ingredient. If you follow the step-by-step direction you're virtually guaranteed success!"

—RICK DeLUCA, Regional Owner WA, OR, NV, CA & HI, EXIT Realty Pacific West

"Nick Krautter's *The Golden Handoff* brings a solution to two serious questions that the real estate industry faces.

**Question 1:** How does an agent that is ready to retire or move on to something else, best take care of the clients that he or she will no longer be serving, while continuing to get paid for the business that he or she has built?

**Answer:** *The Golden Handoff.*

**Question 2:** How does an ambitious agent quickly grow a warm-market, referral-based business?

**Answer:** *The Golden Handoff.*"

—JUSTIN STODDART, Host of the Think Bigger Real Estate Show, Author of *The Upstream Model*

"If you are blessed enough to be in the real estate industry long enough you need to read this book several times. You never know what opportunities will arise and you will want to be ready."

—LISA ARCHER, Leukemia & Lymphoma Society Woman of the Year Candidate, Chief Opportunity Officer, Keller Williams Live Love Homes

# The Golden Handoff Workbook

by Nick Krautter

Real Estate Business Press, Portland 97232

Editing and book design by Indigo: Editing, Design, and More

Printed in the United States of America.

ISBN 978-0-9968146-3-8

# Welcome to the Golden Handoff Workbook!

Whether you're a Retiring Agent or an Adopting Agent, the goal of this workbook is to help you through each step of the Golden Handoff process. Like the relay race analogy in the book, each agent has some simple but important steps to take to make sure you both win the race.

This workbook begins with an at-a-glance checklist for both agents, and then the book is separated into two parts, first for the Retiring Agent and second for the Adopting Agent. Each part features a checklist for that agent and breaks down the process for that person's role.

All activities featured in this workbook are expanded upon in *The Golden Handoff* book, and further resources are listed at the back of the workbook.

With the Golden Handoff Workbook, you have all the steps laid out for you in an easy format so you can make a successful and prosperous handoff.

—Nick Krautter, Author

# Combined Checklist

★ = retiring agents and adopting agents do this worksheet together

# Part I

## The Retiring Agent

### Checklist

| | Task | Date Started | Date Completed |
|---|---|---|---|
| **Step 1** | ☐ Self-Evaluation | _____ | _____ |
| | ☐ Adopting Agents List | _____ | _____ |
| | ☐ Adopting Agent Evaluation | _____ | _____ |
| **Step 2** | ☐ Database Preparation | _____ | _____ |
| | ☐ The Golden Handoff Calculator ★ | _____ | _____ |
| **Step 3** | ☐ Choose a Level of Involvement | _____ | _____ |
| | ☐ Staying Connected | _____ | _____ |
| **Step 4** | ☐ Contract ★ | _____ | _____ |
| **Step 5** | ☐ Marketing Checklist ★ | _____ | _____ |
| **Step 6** | ☐ Database Interview ★ | _____ | _____ |
| | ☐ Systems | _____ | _____ |
| **Step 7** | ☐ Handoff Timeline ★ | _____ | _____ |
| | ☐ Retiring Agent Letter ★ | _____ | _____ |
| **Step 8** | ☐ Letting Go | _____ | _____ |
| | ☐ Winning the Race ★ | _____ | _____ |

★ = retiring agents and adopting agents do this worksheet together

# Step 1

## Self-Evaluation

What do my clients most appreciate about me?

_____

_____


Where does my business come from?

_____

_____


Percent of closings from repeat and referral clients:_____

Average commission per sale: _____

## Adopting Agents List

### *Your Potential Adopting Agents*

Name: _____

Why this person? _____

Name: _____

Why this person? _____

Name: _____

Why this person? _____

Now that you have chosen some candidates to consider for your Adopting Agent, let's dig deeper and interview them on who they are, where their business comes from, and if you think they will be the best fit for adopting your clients. If the Adopting Agent has a team, I recommend meeting the team members who will be calling and meeting with your clients. The following are interview pages for potential Adopting Agents.

## Adopting Agent Evaluation

**Agent Name:** _____

Current Production: _____   Repeat & Referral %: _____

Experience: _____
_____

Relationship Building: _____
_____

Resources: _____
_____

Ethics: _____
_____

Energy: _____
_____

Additional Questions:

1. _____
_____

2. _____
_____

3. _____
_____

## Adopting Agent Evaluation

**Agent Name:** _____

Current Production: _____     Repeat & Referral %: _____

Experience: _____
_____

Relationship Building: _____
_____

Resources: _____
_____

Ethics: _____
_____

Energy: _____
_____

Additional Questions:

1._____
_____

2. _____
_____

3. _____
_____

## Adopting Agent Evaluation

**Agent Name:** _____

Current Production: _____ Repeat & Referral %: _____

Experience: _____
_____

Relationship Building: _____
_____

Resources: _____
_____

Ethics: _____
_____

Energy: _____
_____

Additional Questions:

1. _____
_____

2. _____
_____

3. _____
_____

# Step 2

## Database Preparation

The more accurate and updated my database is, the better the results for me and my Adopting Agent. My database contains:

☐ A list of all my transactions

*Notes:* _____

_____

☐ Each person in my database has the following critical information:

- Name
- Phone number
- Email address
- Address
- Category: A, B, C, and/or descriptive tags (ex., Buyer, Seller, Builder, Investor)

I have documented my marketing plan:

☐ Follow-up/contact timeline

I contact past clients every _____ months.

☐ Events hosted

I host _____ events annually for clients.

☐ I have confirmed the contact information for each person in my database.

☐ I have exported my database into an Excel/CSV format.

## The Golden Handoff Calculator

This page will help you predict how much income you can expect. Also check out Goldenhandoff.com/calculator for an easier way to do this math.

### *Direct Income*

The business contains _____ clients and is _____ % repeat and referral.

_____ clients x _____ % repeat/referral = _____ repeat and referral clients

_____ repeat and referral clients / 10 years = _____ closings per year

_____ closings x $ _____ average commission = $ _____ per year gross

First year is _____ / _____ split

Adopting Agent makes $ _____ from direct income in the first year, and the Retiring Agent receives $ _____ from those transactions.

### *Ongoing Referrals*

Retiring Agent will continue to receive _____ % (typically 20%) from referrals as long as a license is maintained.

_____ referrals per year x $ _____ average commission x _____ % = $ _____ in additional referral income for the Retiring Agent

**In the first year, the Retiring Agent can expect to make $ _____.**

# Step 3

## Choose a Level of Involvement

Before I retire, I will:

1. Deliver a complete database and go over my database with my Adopting Agent.
2. Call my top clients to let them know the Adopting Agent is taking over.
3. Sign the announcement letters the Adopting Agent will send for me on my letterhead and with my return address on the envelopes.

☐ Stop here? I am **totally done.**

4. Re-endorse the Adopting Agent and their work when needed.
5. Keep an ear out for new clients and opportunities.
6. Maintain lead-generation websites and systems.

☐ Stop here? I am **a delegator.**

7. Qualify new clients and set client expectations.
8. Communicate marketing efforts with the Adopting Agent.
9. Call past clients once a year.

☐ I am **a consultant.**

## Staying Connected
Select which level of involvement you plan to keep for each contact method.

### Email
☐ I will continue to monitor my email.
☐ I will forward all emails to the Adopting Agent.

### Phone
☐ I will continue to answer my phone.
☐ I will forward my client-facing number to the Adopting Agent.
☐ I will turn off my number completely (not recommended).

### Website
☐ I will keep my website functioning.
☐ I will transfer the domain to the Adopting Agent.
☐ I will shut down my website altogether.

$ _____ average commission x 30% first-year split =

**$ _____ from even just one referral or inquiry!**

# Step 4

## Contract

Once you've picked your Adopting Agent, you review and sign the contract. Following is a sample contract, so make sure you have your attorney review and approve before you sign. Review the "Contract" chapter in *The Golden Handoff* book for some suggestions on these additional factors you might want to include in your agreement.

Assets

_____

_____

Wild Cards

_____

_____

Exceptions

_____

_____

## *Sample Contract*

Date: _____

Retiring Agent (_____) transfers their client database to _____, under the following terms:

For any purchases or sales by clients in the Retiring Agent database, _____ agrees to pay a referral fee as follows:

Year One:     30% of commissions for properties closed between April 2, 2020, and April 1, 2021
Year Two:     20% of commissions for properties closed between April 2, 2021, and April 1, 2022
Year Three: 10% of commissions for properties closed between April 2, 2022, and April 1, 2023, after which time no referral fees will be due

For new referrals from the Retiring Agent that are not part of the Retiring Agent database, _____ agrees to pay a 20% referral fee for the first transaction by each client for perpetuity as long as the Retiring Agent is legally licensed to receive referral fees.

Exceptions: _____

Assets: All soft assets (ex., website, work email and phone numbers, marketing templates) to be transferred to _____. Hard assets (ex., lockboxes, equipment) to be negotiated for sale at fair market value.

Retiring Agent agrees to the following duties:

1. Maintain a real estate license with the appropriate status to continue to receive referral income.
2. Communicate any inquiries by database clients and new leads to _____ and to endorse _____ to database clients and new leads.

_____ agrees to the following duties:

1. Maintain a high level of marketing and follow-up procedures with database clients.
2. Communicate new business as well as pending and closed sales with the Retiring Agent.
3. Pay for all marketing and maintain a business that can support the real estate needs of the database.

_____          _____
Retiring Agent Signature                              Date

_____          _____
Adopting Agent Signature                              Date

# Step 5

## Marketing Checklist

You and your Adopting Agent fill this out separately and then compare your marketing plans. The secret to success is consistent marketing.

### *What Is My Big Why?*

_____

_____

_____

Channel is how you contact.
Message is what you say.
Frequency is how many times a year you contact.

### *Mailings*

I do physical mailings _____ times per year.

### *Phone*

I call past clients _____ times per year.

### *In-Person*

I host client events _____ times per year.

### *Email*

I email all clients _____ times per year.

## Social Media

I use the following channels:

- ☐ Facebook
- ☐ Twitter
- ☐ Instagram
- ☐ LinkedIn
- ☐ Other: _____

and post _____ times weekly.

I have_____ followers.

## Accountability

Together, we will hold accountability meetings _____ (frequency).

## Notes

_____

_____

_____

# Step 6

## Database Interview

A critical step is to meet with the Adopting Agent and go over your entire database. I like to print out the basic info—Name, Phone, Email, and Address—in an Excel spreadsheet and share information about each client in the database. The Adopting Agent will ask questions, and the goal is to best get to know the clients they're about to adopt and see who might need help now versus in the future.

### *Leads vs. Clients*

The most important information in a database is that of the actual clients—people who have bought, sold, or referred clients to the Retiring Agent. But most successful agents have leads in their database as well. Leads are anyone you think might be a potential client that has working contact info. If you have internet leads with bad emails or who have unsubscribed, they should probably be deleted. Leads with contact info are worth staying in touch with, but you can't expect the Adopting Agent to invest the same time that actual clients will receive.

### *Database Notes*

_____

_____

## Systems

Complete this chart about the systems you currently have in place and the purpose they serve. You will want to go over this with the Adopting Agent to make sure they can integrate them with their own systems in order to effectively maintain contact with clients and organization after the handoff.

| System | Use |
|---|---|
| | *CRM* |
| | *Email Platform* |
| | *Printing Company* |
| | *Sign/Install Company* |
| | *File System/Records* |
| | |
| | |

# Step 7

## Handoff Timeline

The database will transfer as of _____. At that point, the rest of the handoff will follow this timeline:

1. The letter from the Retiring Agent will be sent via email and USPS to all clients in the database _____ days before the official retirement date.
2. Top clients will be called _____ days before the letter is sent by the Retiring Agent.
3. Remaining clients will be called within _____ days after the letter is sent by the Retiring Agent.
4. The announcement will be made on both agents' social media _____ days after the letter is sent.
5. A retirement party will be hosted within _____ weeks of the letter being sent.
6. Adopting Agent will call top clients within 1 week of retirement date using the Adopting Agent script. All clients will be called within 3 weeks of retirement date.
7. Adopting Agent will now have all adopted clients in their marketing plan for ongoing newsletters, calls, event invites, etc.

*Notes*

_____

_____

_____

_____

_____

_____

_____

_____

## Retiring Agent Letter

Use this Golden Handoff sample letter/email as a template to write your Retiring Agent letter to clients. The letter will go on your letterhead, and the Adopting Agent will send it out for you.

October 5, 2020

Hi, everyone,

As you may have heard, my wife and I are heading to Los Angeles for some time to work in the movie scene. As we may be there for one year or longer, we are proud to announce our partnership with one of the top real estate teams in Portland to provide excellent service to you while we are gone. This will also allow us to be consultants to Nick and his team for all of you.

The team is led by Nick Krautter, who is one of the top agents in the city and also the real estate expert for News Radio 101 FM – KXL. Nick's team sold an impressive ninety-seven properties in 2019!

Please always feel free to call me with questions, as my phone numbers won't change and our website will still be available to you, but rest assured that you are in very capable hands with Nick and his team while we are away. In addition to our weekly "Best Deals in Portland" email, you will also start receiving Nick's Client Information Plan, which will provide accurate, local information about our real estate market. In the meantime, when you or someone you know is thinking of buying or selling real estate, give us a call.

Sincerely,
David Belmont
Nick Krautter

# Step 8

## Letting Go

### *Setting Expectations*

I expect _____ deals per year from my database.

### *Metrics and Accountability*

I have the following expectations of the Adopting Agent each month, which will be covered during each accountability check-in:

_____

_____

_____

### *Feedback*

I will ask for feedback or testimonials from my past clients regarding the Adopting Agent within _____ weeks of the transition. I will provide this feedback or any concerns to the Adopting Agent.

### *Hurdles for the Retiring Agent*

Some potential hurdles that I may encounter are:

_____

_____

_____

_____

I will overcome these hurdles by:

_____

_____

_____

_____

# Winning the Race

*Important Milestones*

_____

_____

_____

_____

_____

_____

_____

*Notes About Our Journey*

_____

_____

_____

_____

_____

_____

_____

# Part II

## The Adopting Agent

### Checklist

| | Task | Date Started | Date Completed |
|---|---|---|---|
| **Step 1** | ☐ Retiring Agents List | | |
| | ☐ Marketing to Retiring Agents | | |
| **Step 2** | ☐ The Golden Handoff Calculator ★ | | |
| **Step 3** | ☐ Relax! This is for the Retiring Agent. | | |
| **Step 4** | ☐ Contract ★ | | |
| **Step 5** | ☐ Marketing Checklist ★ | | |
| **Step 6** | ☐ Database Interview ★ | | |
| | ☐ Systems | | |
| **Step 7** | ☐ Handoff Timeline ★ | | |
| | ☐ Retiring Agent Letter ★ | | |
| **Step 8** | ☐ Hurdles | | |
| | ☐ Winning the Race ★ | | |

★ = retiring agents and adopting agents do this worksheet together

# Step 1

## Retiring Agents List

### *Agents I Know Whose Clients I Want to Adopt*

1. _____

2. _____

3. _____

4. _____

5. _____

### *Production Analysis*

I want to market to agents who have been in business for more than _____ years.

I have noticed a drop in production in these top agents: _____

_____

### *Notes*

_____

☐ I've spoken with my broker, lender, title rep, and other vendors to let them know that I want to adopt clients.

## Marketing to Retiring Agents

*Stay* in touch, *share* your successes, and *ask* for business.

### My Marketing Plan

Use this checklist to help grow your business through Retiring Agents:

- ☐ Ship copies of *The Golden Handoff* book to _____ potentially Retiring Agents.
- ☐ Send emails to potential Retiring Agents.
- ☐ Send postcards to potential Retiring Agents.
- ☐ Collect testimonials from Retiring Agents I'm currently working with.
- ☐ Add _____ new leads to my CRM weekly.

# Step 2

## The Golden Handoff Calculator

This page will help you predict how much income you can expect. Also check out Goldenhandoff
.com/calculator for an easier way to do this math.

### *Direct Income*

The business contains _____ clients and is _____ % repeat and referral.

_____ clients x _____% repeat/referral = _____ repeat and referral clients

_____ repeat and referral clients / 10 years = _____ closings per year

_____ closings x $ _____ average commission = $ _____ per year gross

First year is _____ / _____ split

Adopting Agent makes $ _____ from direct income in the first year, and the Retiring Agent receives
$ _____ from those transactions.

### *Ongoing Referrals*

Retiring Agent will continue to receive _____ % (typically 20%) from new referrals as long as
license is maintained, so you'll get 80%.

_____ new referrals per year x $ _____ average commission x _____% = $ _____ in additional
referral income for the Adopting Agent

**In the first year, the Adopting Agent can expect to make $ _____.**

### *Indirect Income*

_____ % of my closed deals are usually listings.

_____ closings per year expected from above.

Assuming each listing creates enough leads to expect one closed sale,
$ _____ average commission x ( _____% x _____ deals) = $ _____ indirect income

### *Adopted Client Referrals*

_____ clients adopted x 25% closed referrals = _____ adopted client referrals

_____ adopted client referrals / 10 years = _____ deals per year

$ _____ average commission x _____ referral deals per year = $ _____ income

**I, as the Adopting Agent, can expect to make an additional $ _____ per year from new leads from listings and referrals from the Retiring Agent's database.**

# Step 3

## Relax!

This step is for the Retiring Agent. Right now they are making important decisions about their ongoing level of involvement and updating their database so you have updated contact info and notes on all the clients you're about to adopt. If the Retiring Agent doesn't want to do this step, then plan for more time during the database interview (Step 6).

# Step 4

## Contract

Once you and the Retiring Agent have decided to work together, you agree on the contract and then the fun begins! Following is a sample contract, so make sure you have your attorney review and approve before you sign. Review the "Contract" chapter in *The Golden Handoff* book for some suggestions on these additional factors you might want to include in your agreement.

Assets

_____

_____

Wild Cards

_____

_____

Exceptions

_____

_____

## *Sample Contract*

Date: _____

Retiring Agent (_____) transfers their client database to _____ under the following terms:

For any purchases or sales by clients in the Retiring Agent database, _____ agrees to pay a referral fee as follows:

Year One: 30% of commissions for properties closed between April 2, 2020, and April 1, 2021
Year Two: 20% of commissions for properties closed between April 2, 2021, and April 1, 2022
Year Three: 10% of commissions for properties closed between April 2, 2022, and April 1, 2023, after which time no referral fees will be due

For new referrals from the Retiring Agent that are not part of the Retiring Agent database, _____ agrees to pay a 20% referral fee for the first transaction by each client for perpetuity as long as the Retiring Agent is legally licensed to receive referral fees.

Exceptions: _____

Assets: All soft assets (ex., website, work email and phone numbers, marketing templates) to be transferred to _____. Hard assets (ex., lockboxes, equipment) to be negotiated for sale at fair market value.

Retiring Agent agrees to the following duties:

1. Maintain a real estate license with the appropriate status to continue to receive referral income.
2. Communicate any inquiries by database clients and new leads to _____ and to endorse _____ to database clients and new leads.

_____ agrees to the following duties:

1. Maintain a high level of marketing and follow-up procedures with database clients.
2. Communicate new business as well as pending and closed sales with the Retiring Agent.
3. Pay for all marketing and maintain a business that can support the real estate needs of the database.


_____          _____
Retiring Agent Signature                 Date


_____          _____
Adopting Agent Signature                 Date

# Step 5

## Marketing Checklist

You and your Retiring Agent fill this out separately and then compare your marketing plans. The secret to success is consistent marketing.

### *What Is My Big Why?*

_____

Channel is how you contact.
Message is what you say.
Frequency is how many times a year you contact.

### *Mailings*
I do physical mailings _____ times per year.

### *Phone*
I call past clients _____ times per year.

### *In-Person*
I host client events _____ times per year.

### *Email*
I email all clients _____ times per year.

### *Social Media*
I use the following channels:

☐ Facebook
☐ Twitter
☐ Instagram
☐ LinkedIn
☐ Other:_____

and post _____times weekly.

I have _____ followers.

## Accountability

Together, we will hold accountability meetings _____ (frequency).

## Notes

_____

_____

_____

# Step 6

## Database Interview

A critical step is to meet with the Retiring Agent and go over their entire database. I like to print out the basic info—Name, Phone, Email, and Address—in an Excel spreadsheet and ask questions about each client in the database. Some sample questions are below, but feel free to add more or change these. The goal is to best get to know the new clients you're about to adopt and see who might need you now versus in the future.

- Do they currently own?
- What do they like to invest in and how often?
- Do they refer friends, family, and coworkers to you?
- When are they planning on selling and making a move?
- How did you meet them?

### *Leads vs. Clients*

The most important information in a database is that of the actual clients—people who have bought, sold, or referred clients to the Retiring Agent. But most successful agents have leads in their database as well. Leads are anyone you think might be a potential client that has working contact info. If you have internet leads with bad emails or who have unsubscribed, they should probably be deleted. Make sure you have a different marketing plan for leads. You can't love everyone the same, and you want to focus your attention on clients.

### *Database Notes*

_____

_____

_____

## Systems

Complete this chart about the systems you currently have in place and the purpose they serve. Then discuss the Retiring Agent's systems to make sure you can integrate them with your own systems in order to effectively maintain contact with clients after the handoff.

| System | Use |
|---|---|
| | CRM |
| | Email Platform |
| | Printing Company |
| | Sign/Install Company |
| | File System/Records |
| | |
| | |

# Step 7

## Handoff Timeline

The database will transfer as of _____. At that point, the rest of the handoff will follow this timeline:

1. The letter from the Retiring Agent will be sent via email and USPS to all clients in the database _____ days before the official retirement date.
2. Top clients will be called by the Retiring Agent _____ days before the letter is sent.
3. Remaining clients will be called by the Retiring Agent within _____ days.
4. The announcement will be made on both agents' social media _____ days after the letter is sent.
5. A retirement party will be hosted within _____ weeks of the letter being sent.
6. Adopting Agent will call top clients within 1 week of retirement date using the Adopting Agent script. All clients will be called within 3 weeks of retirement date.
7. Adopting Agent will now have all adopted clients in their marketing plan for ongoing newsletters, calls, event invites etc.

### Notes

_____

_____

_____

_____

_____

_____

_____

_____

## Retiring Agent Letter

The Retiring Agent will use this Golden Handoff sample letter/email as a template to write their Retiring Agent letter to clients. The letter will be on their letterhead, and you will mail it out for them.

October 5, 2020

Hi, everyone,

As you may have heard, my wife and I are heading to Los Angeles for some time to work in the movie scene. As we may be there for one year or longer, we are proud to announce our partnership with one of the top real estate teams in Portland to provide excellent service to you while we are gone. This will also allow us to be consultants to Nick and his team for all of you.

The team is led by Nick Krautter, who is one of the top agents in the city and also the real estate expert for News Radio 101 FM – KXL. Despite the challenging market, Nick's team sold an impressive ninety-seven properties in 2019!

Please always feel free to call me with questions, as my phone numbers won't change and our website will still be available to you, but rest assured that you are in very capable hands with Nick and his team while we are away. In addition to our weekly "Best Deals in Portland" email, you will also start receiving Nick's Client Information Plan, which will provide accurate, local information about our real estate market. In the meantime, when you or someone you know is thinking of buying or selling real estate, give us a call.

Sincerely,
David Belmont
Nick Krautter

# Step 8

## Hurdles

Some potential hurdles that I may encounter are:

_____

_____

_____


I will overcome these hurdles by:

_____

_____

_____

# Winning the Race

*Important Milestones*

_____

_____

_____

*Notes About Our Journey*

_____

_____

_____

# Resources

This section provides at-a-glance resources to help you on your way. For exclusive access to editable copies of all documents referenced in the workbook, including scripts, letters, and contracts, sign up at Goldenhandoff.com.

### *Want to Get More Golden?*

☐ Join our Facebook Group: The Golden Handoff.
☐ Stay tuned for the Golden Handoff Academy training program.
☐ Have Nick speak live at your event.
☐ Host a LIVE webinar with Nick for your group.

To find out more, email Nick@goldenhandoff.com.

## The Golden Handoff Calculator

This page will help you predict how much income you can expect. Also check out Goldenhandoff .com/calculator for an easier way to do this math.

### Direct Income

The business contains _____ clients and is _____ % repeat and referral.

_____ clients x _____% repeat/referral = _____ repeat and referral clients

_____ repeat and referral clients / 10 years = _____ closings per year

_____ closings x $ _____ average commission = $ _____ per year gross

First year is _____ / _____ split

Adopting Agent makes $ _____ from direct income in the first year, and the Retiring Agent receives $ _____ from those transactions.

### Ongoing Referrals

Retiring Agent will continue to receive _____ % (typically 20%) from new referrals as long as license is maintained, so you'll get 80%.

_____ new referrals per year x $ _____ average commission x _____% = $ _____ in additional referral income for the Adopting Agent

**In the first year, the Adopting Agent can expect to make $ _____.**

### Indirect Income

_____ % of my closed deals are usually listings.

_____ closings per year expected from above.

Assuming each listing creates enough leads to expect one closed sale,
$ _____ average commission x ( _____% x _____ deals) = $ _____ indirect income

### *Adopted Client Referrals*

_____ clients adopted x 25% closed referrals = _____ adopted client referrals

_____ adopted client referrals / 10 years = _____ deals per year

$ _____ average commission x _____ referral deals per year = $ _____ income

**I, as the Adopting Agent, can expect to make an additional $ _____ per year from new leads from listings and referrals from the Retiring Agent's database.**

# Scripts

## Script for First Call to Adopted Clients

Hi, this is Nick Krautter with City & State Real Estate. I promised your Realtor, John, I'd call and check in to see if you had any real estate questions or needs I can help with.

—Yes.

[Then take notes and set appointment.]

[or]

—No.

Perfect, most people are very happy with their homes. Did you know that the market is up 10% over last year?

—Wow, I didn't know that.

I'll be staying in touch, and you'll get my newsletter and monthly market emails. Thanks for taking my call, I look forward to helping you, so let me know if you need anything at all, even just a referral for a plumber, etc. Before I let you go, I want to ask, who do you know that might be buying or selling that I can be of service to?

## Script for Approaching Potential Retiring Agents

Hi, John, this is Nick Krautter over at City & State Real Estate. I really enjoyed working with you on our last deal. [If you haven't done a deal with them: "I've heard so many good things about you and have always admired your business."] I recently read an amazing book about how to retire from real estate and wanted to chat with you about it. What is your plan for your business when you decide to retire from real estate?

—I don't want to retire yet.

Great, I'd love to give you a copy of the book and talk about the strategies of how to prepare now and make more money when you do decide to retire. Would you be interested in netting an extra $100,000 after you retire?

[or]

—I'm going to just wind down.

That's what I was going to do too until I learned I could net an extra $100,000 *after* I retire if I do a Golden Handoff and not just wind down. Do you have 20 minutes to meet for coffee and talk about how I can help you retire, make more money, and make sure your clients are taken care of?

# Letters and Contracts

## *Retiring Agent Letter*

October 5, 2020

Hi, everyone,

As you may have heard, my wife and I are heading to Los Angeles for some time to work in the movie scene. As we may be there for one year or longer, we are proud to announce our partnership with one of the top real estate teams in Portland to provide excellent service to you while we are gone. This will also allow us to be consultants to Nick and his team for all of you.

The team is led by Nick Krautter, who is one of the top agents in the city and also the real estate expert for News Radio 101 FM – KXL. Despite the challenging market, Nick's team sold an impressive ninety-seven properties in 2019!

Please always feel free to call me with questions, as my phone numbers won't change and our website will still be available to you, but rest assured that you are in very capable hands with Nick and his team while we are away. In addition to our weekly "Best Deals in Portland" email, you will also start receiving Nick's Client Information Plan, which will provide accurate, local information about our real estate market. In the meantime, when you or someone you know is thinking of buying or selling real estate, give us a call.

Sincerely,
David Belmont
Nick Krautter

## Sample Contract

Date: _____

Retiring Agent (_____) transfers their client database to _____ under the following terms:

For any purchases or sales by clients in the Retiring Agent database, _____ agrees to pay a referral fee as follows:

Year One: 30% of commissions for properties closed between April 2, 2020, and April 1, 2021

Year Two: 20% of commissions for properties closed between April 2, 2021, and April 1, 2022

Year Three: 10% of commissions for properties closed between April 2, 2022, and April 1, 2023, after which time no referral fees will be due

For new referrals from the Retiring Agent that are not part of the Retiring Agent database, _____ agrees to pay a 20% referral fee for the first transaction by each client for perpetuity as long as the Retiring Agent is legally licensed to receive referral fees.

Exceptions: _____

Assets: All soft assets (ex., website, work email and phone numbers, marketing templates) to be transferred to _____. Hard assets (ex., lockboxes, equipment) to be negotiated for sale at fair market value.

Retiring Agent agrees to the following duties:

1. Maintain a real estate license with the appropriate status to continue to receive referral income.
2. Communicate any inquiries by database clients and new leads to _____ and to endorse _____ to database clients and new leads.

_____ agrees to the following duties:

1. Maintain a high level of marketing and follow-up procedures with database clients.
2. Communicate new business as well as pending and closed sales with the Retiring Agent.
3. Pay for all marketing and maintain a business that can support the real estate needs of the database.


_____                    _____
Retiring Agent Signature                       Date


_____                    _____
Adopting Agent Signature                       Date

## Handout for Retiring Agents

Want to retire from real estate with relaxation and free time? Want to maintain an income stream *and* ensure your clients are well taken care of? You can do it! It's called the Golden Handoff, and here's how it works:

1. You connect with a successful agent to adopt your clients. This person is your Adopting Agent.
2. You announce your retirement and that the Adopting Agent will be taking care of your clients going forward.
3. The Adopting Agent calls, emails, and proactively communicates with your clients.
4. You collect referral fees on any closed deals with your clients for the next three years!

When most agents retire, they don't get anything from the effort and time they've put into their business. You might get a referral or two you can send to a peer, but the problem is, there is no proactive effort.

The Golden Handoff is the process of finding a great Adopting Agent who will take over the task of marketing to your clients and make sure you get the most benefit from all the work you've put into your business. I was able to help one Retiring Agent make $50,000 in referral fees in one year!

Don't let your business just disappear. Take the few simple steps in the Golden Handoff, and you'll be making money long after you stop working!

I would love to talk with you about how I can help you retire and still make money and ensure your clients are well cared for!

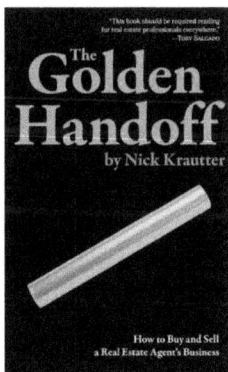

Yours,
Nick Krautter
nick@goldenhandoff.com
503.901.8100

# About the Author

# Nick Krautter

Nick Krautter is the author of *The Golden Handoff: How to Buy and Sell a Real Estate Agent's Business*, which debuted at number one on Amazon for mergers and acquisitions. His goal is to teach real estate agents how to grow their businesses and to help them later retire and benefit from their years of hard work.

Since 2006 Nick has been a Realtor in Portland, Oregon, where he leads a team and frequently serves as a real estate expert for the media. Krautter is an avid golfer, writer, reader, and talker who enjoys all the food, drink, and adventures that can be found in the great Northwest.

He is unusually tall and once lived on a sailboat. He loves his job and still gets up early, excited about what each day holds.

www.ingramcontent.com/pod-product-compliance
Lightning Source LLC
Chambersburg PA
CBHW081748200326

41597CB00024B/4437